The Vibrant Violin

Music Theory
Book 1

A theory book especially for violin players

covering Grades 1-2

All the basics to get you going.

Easy to follow explanations,

puzzles and more.

All with the beginner violin player in mind.

Amanda Oosthuizen

Jemima Oosthuizen

The Vibrant Violin Series

Wild Music Publications

www.wildmusicpublications.com

We hope you enjoy *The Vibrant Violin Music Theory Book 1.*

Take a look at our other exciting books, including: 50+ Greatest Classics, Catch the Beat, Christmas Duets, Easy Tunes from Around the World, Trick or Treat – A Halloween Suite, Champagne and Chocolate, Fish 'n' Ships, and many more solo and duet books.

For more info on other amazing books, please go to:

WildMusicPublications.com

Visit our secret page for a **free backing track,** and more fun things for free! visit:

http://WildMusicPublications.com/725secret-violin-track942k/

And use the password: **m@dStrings4U!**

Happy Music Making!

The Wild Music Publications Team

To keep up –to-date with our new releases, why not **follow us on Twitter**

@WMPublications

To play the Violin well, you need to read music and understand the mysteries of music theory. The Vibrant Violin Music Theory Book 1 includes all the basics you'll need up to Grade 2 Violin and is written with the beginner Violin player in mind. Take it slowly, complete a little bit at a time and have fun!

Each section explains a new aspect of music in an easy-to-read way and is followed by exercises and puzzles to help you remember what you've learnt.

 Writing activities are shown by a Violin pencil.

After several sections, you will find a Check page where you can see how much you have remembered and keep score.

At the end of the book, there are Violin information pages, more puzzles, a list of musical terms and symbols and a chart where you can keep a record of the sections you have completed.

If you want to check your **ANSWERS**, a free answer book download is available on the **SECRET VIOLIN PAGE** of our website. Find out how to get there on the second page of the book.

When you have finished, take a look at Book 2. It includes all the crazy theory you need to know from Grades 3 – 5 Violin including: ornaments, more Violin facts, making scales, compound time signatures and much more.

Contents

Accidentals 16

Arpeggios 38

Certificate 53

Check 1 12

Check 2 21

Check 3 31

Check 4 40

Check 5 46

Degrees of the Scale 32

Dizzy Demon 45

Dotted Crotchets 28

Final Check 51

Interesting Violin Facts 50

Intervals................................... 33

Key Signatures......................... 24

Ledger Lines............................. 20

Letter Names............................. 3

Major Scales.......................... 22

Minor Scales......................... 35

More Major Scales.................. 26

Musical Symbols.................... 41

Musical Terms....................... 42

Note Values 7

Quavers 18

Repeats and Directions 44

Rests 11

Stems 10

The String Family.................. 49

The Violin........................... 47

The Violin Family.................. 48

The Violinist's Progress 52

Time Signatures 13

Treble Clef 2

Treble Clef

Violin music is written in treble clef.

Treble clef is also called G clef.

Music is written on five lines called a stave (or staff).

The treble clef is drawn at the start of every stave.

Stave

Music is divided into bars by bar lines.

Draw a treble clef in every bar. It may help to start by curling around a dot on the second line.

The end of a section of music is shown by a double bar line.

The end of a piece of music is shown by a final bar line.

Phrase

A phrase is a short section of music that makes sense, rather like a sentence.

Phrases are shown by a large slur.

Phrases are often four bars long.

Letter Names

Notes are written on the lines and in the spaces.

The lower sounds are at the bottom of the stave.

E F G A B C D E F

Notes in the spaces spell FACE

F A C E

Write the letter names under these notes.

F

example ....

Write these notes in the spaces.

F A C E

Notes on the lines

E G B D F

Every Green Bus Drives Fast

Write the letter names under these notes.

E

example ....

Write your own selection of notes on the lines.

4

✎ *Write the letter names under these notes in the spaces.*

F ....
example

✎ *Write the letter names under these notes on the lines.*

G ....
example

✎ *Write your own selection of notes on lines and in spaces.*

✎ *Write the letter names under these notes on lines and in spaces.*

....

....

....

....

Write the notes in spaces above the letter names.

example

F   C   A   E   F   C   A   F   E   C

Write the notes on lines above the letter names.

example

B   G   E   F   D   E   G   B   D   F

Write the notes on lines or spaces above the letter names.

example

F   G   A   B   B   C   D   E   E   D   C   B

example

A   G   F   E   G   B   D   F   E   C   A   F

Write notes in lines and spaces starting from the bottom of the stave.

Write the letter names beneath the notes.

B
example ....

....

C
example ....

....

6

Write these words in music.

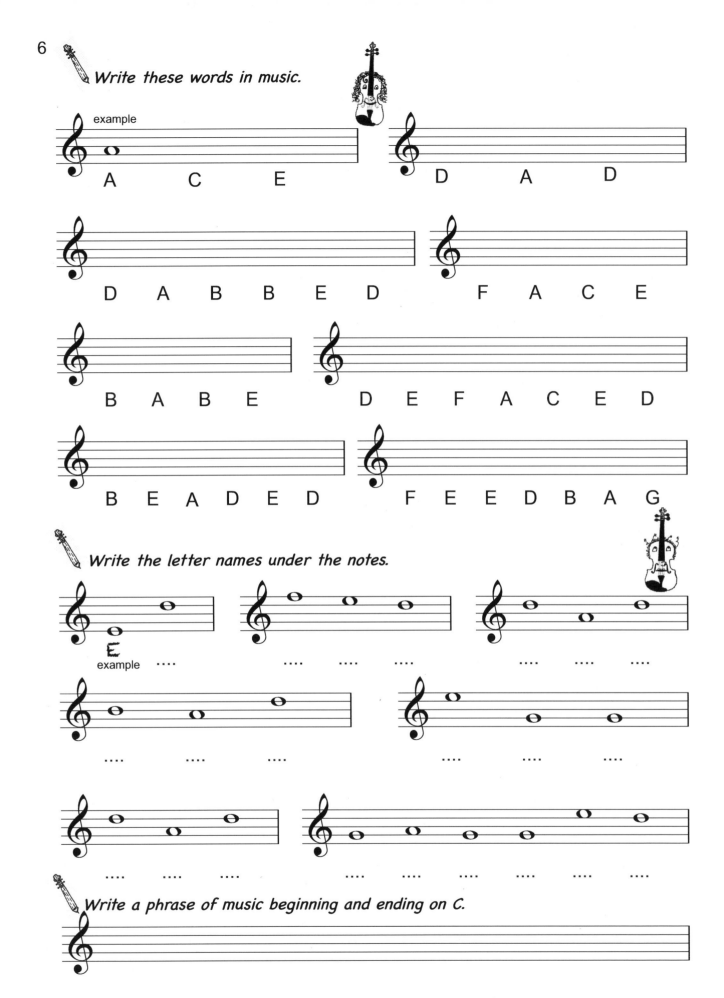

Write the letter names under the notes.

Write a phrase of music beginning and ending on C.

Note Values

Dotted Notes

A dot next to a note adds half its value to that note.

2 + 1 = 3

Semibreve - 4 counts

Write a semibreve in every bar.

4
example

Dotted minim - 3 counts

Write a dotted minim in every bar.

3
example

Minim - 2 counts

Write a minim in every bar.

2
example

Crotchet - 1 count

Write a crotchet in every bar.

1
example

Write a mixed selection of note values on the notes A and B.

8 Write the number of counts.

♩ ♩ o ♩. ♩ ♩ o ♩. ♩ o ♩. ♩

2

example

Ties

A tie is a loop joining notes that are the same. It means add the notes together.

♩ ‿ ♩. = 2 + 3

Write the counts and do the sum.

♩ ♩
2 + 1 = 3
....
example

♩ ♩
.... + ... = ...

♩ ♩
.... + ... = ...

♩ ♩ ♩.
.... + ... + ... = ...

o ♩ ♩
.... + ... + ... = ...

♩. ♩
.... + ... = ...

♩. o
.... + ... = ...

Write in the missing notes below the *.

*
3 counts

*
9 counts

*
5 counts

Write notes that make each bar add up to four crotchets.

Write notes that make each bar add up to three crotchets.

Using G, A, B and C, (all on the stave) write notes of different lengths.

 Match the boxes with the correct number of counts.

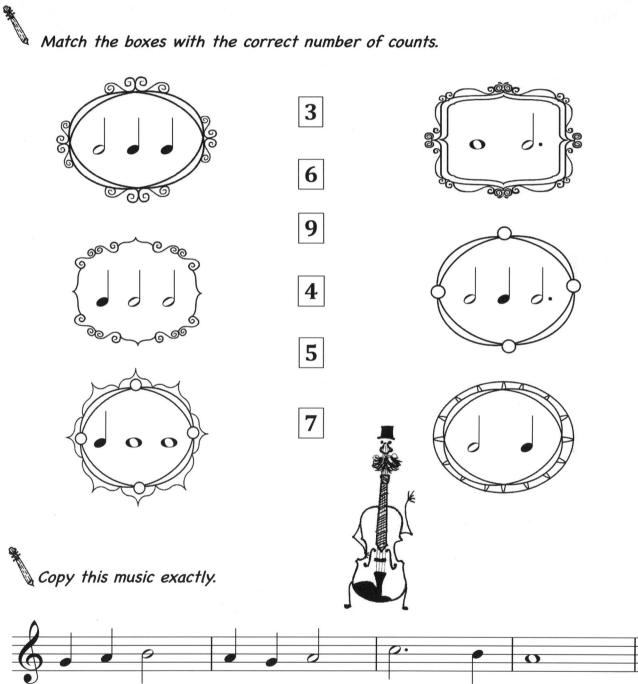

 Copy this music exactly.

Stems

The stems are on the left when they go down.

All notes except semibreves have stems.

The stems are on the right when they go up.

The stem goes down if a note is above the middle line.

The stem goes up if a note is below the middle line.

The stem of D on the middle line can go either up or down.

Add a stem to each of these noteheads.

Write a mixture of low and high noteheads and then add the stems.

Rests

✎ **Check 1** Find out how much you remember.

Mix and Match Match the symbol to its name and number of beats.

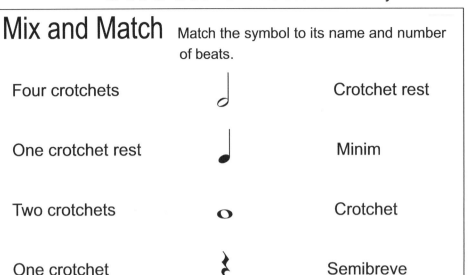

Four crotchets   ♩(minim symbol)   Crotchet rest

One crotchet rest   ♩   Minim

Two crotchets   𝅝   Crotchet

One crotchet   𝄽   Semibreve

Quick Check Are the letters correct. Tick or cross the answers.

G   B   C   E   G   A   F   E   D   A   B   G   C   F   A   A

Quiz True or false? Circle the right answer.

1. Music is divided into bars by bar lines.   True   False

2. Music is written on four lines called a stave.   True   False

3. Music uses the first eight letters of the alphabet.   True   False

4. Violin music is written mostly in bass clef.   True   False

5. A semibreve is worth two minims.   True   False

6. In music silence is shown by rests.   True   False

How many did you get right?

Time Signatures

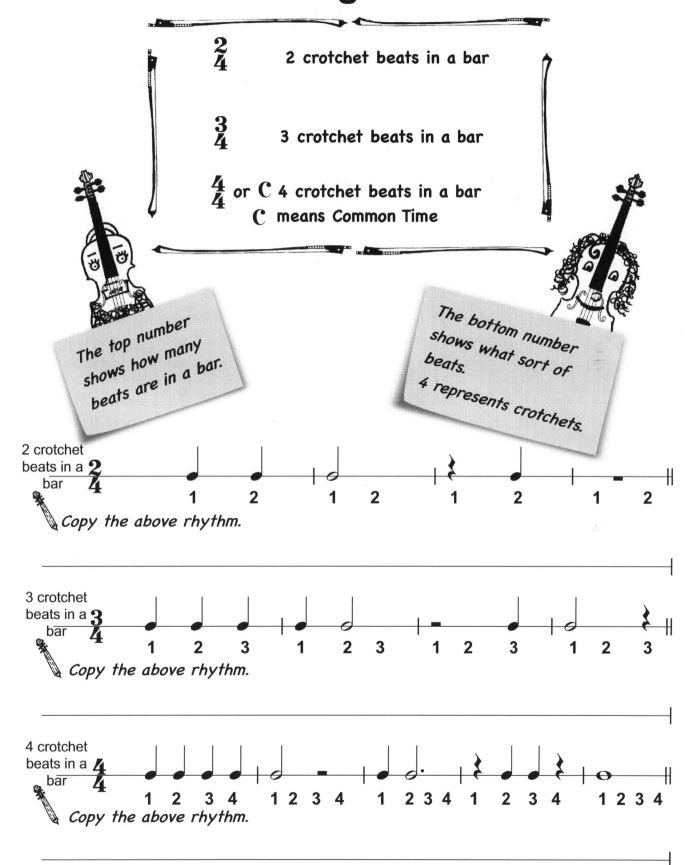

$\frac{2}{4}$ 2 crotchet beats in a bar

$\frac{3}{4}$ 3 crotchet beats in a bar

$\frac{4}{4}$ or **C** 4 crotchet beats in a bar
C means Common Time

The top number shows how many beats are in a bar.

The bottom number shows what sort of beats.
4 represents crotchets.

2 crotchet beats in a bar $\frac{2}{4}$

1   2   1   2   1   2   1   2

Copy the above rhythm.

3 crotchet beats in a bar $\frac{3}{4}$

1   2   3   1   2   3   1   2   3   1   2   3

Copy the above rhythm.

4 crotchet beats in a bar $\frac{4}{4}$

1 2 3 4   1 2 3 4   1 2 3 4   1 2 3 4   1 2 3 4

Copy the above rhythm.

Match the bar with its time signature.

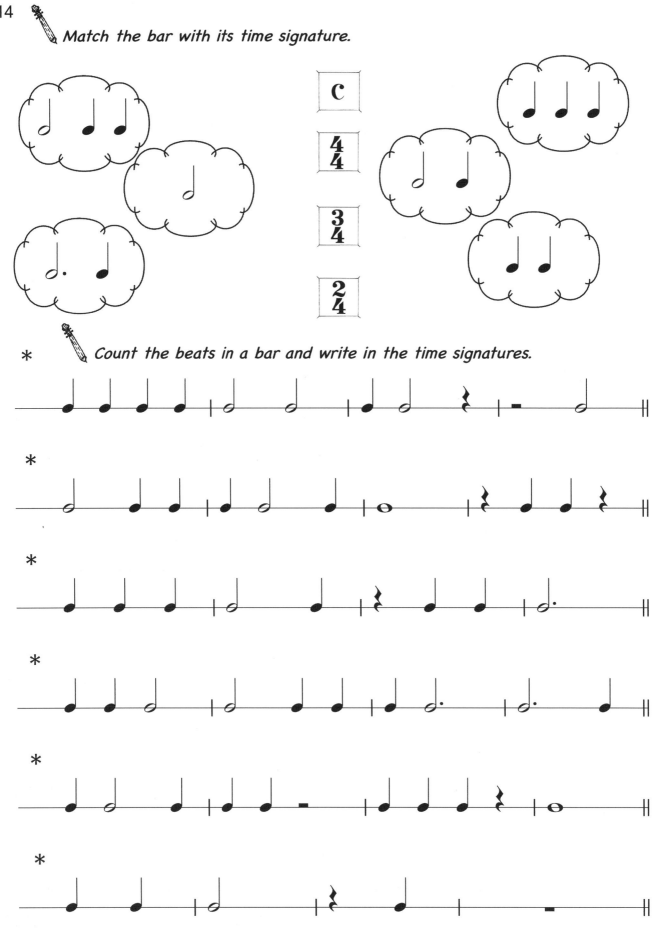

* *Count the beats in a bar and write in the time signatures.*

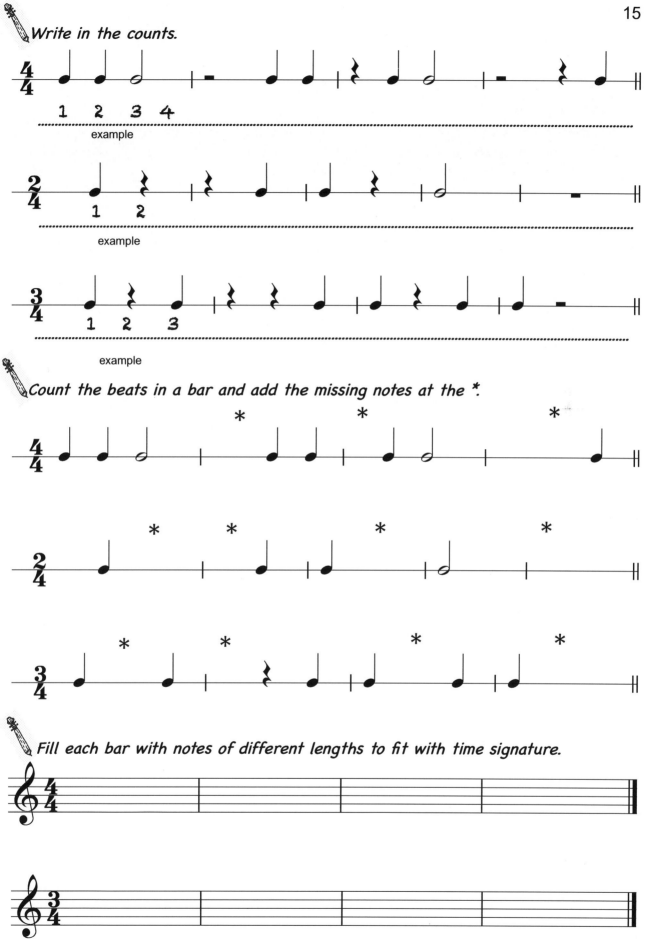

Accidentals

An accidental is a sharp, flat or natural that occurs in a piece of music.

♯ **Sharp**   *A sharp raises a note.*

♭ **Flat**   *A flat lowers a note.*

♮ **Natural**   *A natural restores a note to its original pitch.*

An accidental changes every following note in the bar that is on the same space or line.

An accidental is written in front of a note.

An accidental is written on the same line or in the same space as the note.

Write a sharp before each note.

example

Write a flat before each note.

example

Write a natural before each note.

example

Name the notes.

Name the notes.

Write the notes.

Bb   F#   G#   B♮   Eb   C#   A♮

Gb   D♮   A#   E#   Fb   Db   Cb

Write notes with accidentals but of different lengths so that every bar fits with the time signature.

When notes have the same letter name but are different pitches, another accidental is written.

Name the notes.

G#   G#
example

Write a tune in which every note is a flat.

Write a tune in which every note is a sharp.

Quavers

♪ Quaver ♪

⁊ Quaver rest ⁊

A quaver is half of one crotchet.

The flag is always drawn on the right side of the stem.

Two quavers are usually beamed together to form a crotchet beat.

2 quavers = 1 crotchet

4 quavers = 1 minim

The first and/or last four quavers in a bar can be beamed together if they form half the bar, but never the middle four.

8 quavers = 1 semibreve

Write groups of quavers and crotchets.
Remember to check how many crotchet beats are in a bar.

Fill in the numbers.

A semibreve o = [ ] ♩ minims

A minim ♩ = [ ] ♪ crotchets

A crotchet ♪ = [ ] ♫ quavers

Join the shapes that have the same
number of beats.

Finish off writing in the counts.

1 + 2 + 3 + 4 +   1   2 + 3 + 4

1   2 + 3   4

1   2   3   4

Write notes of different lengths to fit with the time signature. Use any notes.

Ledger Lines

Check 2 How much do you remember?

Mix and Match Match the time signature to its description.

Four crotchets in a bar   2/4

Three crotchets in a bar   4/4

Two crotchets crotchets in a bar 3/4

Quick Check Are the letters correct? Tick or cross the answers.

G F♭ C♯ F   G A A A♭   A A B♭ D   G F♭ E♭ A♯

Quiz True or false? Circle the right answer.

1. Two quavers add up to one crotchet.   True   False

2. Four quavers add up to one minim.   True   False

3. A natural sign is not an accidental.   True   False

4. A time signature's top number tells us what sort of beat is in a bar.

True   False

5. A time signature's bottom number tells us what sort of beat is in a bar.

True   False

How many did you get right?

Major Scales

All major scales have the same tune based on the steps between notes.

The steps that make up a scale are called tones (whole steps) and semitones (half steps).

Scales are a series of notes going up and down in steps.

All major scales have the same pattern of tones and semitones.

An octave is an interval of eight notes. From low C to high C is an octave.

C major scale (one octave) ascending

tone   tone   semitone   tone   tone   tone   semitone

C major scale (one octave) descending

semitone   tone   tone   tone   semitone   tone   tone

Draw a bracket above the semitone intervals.

G major scale (one octave) ascending (F#)

tone   tone   semitone   tone   tone   tone   semitone

D major scale (one octave) ascending (F# and C#)

tone   tone   semitone   tone   tone   tone   semitone

Write in the missing notes and name the scale.

C ....

Copy the scale exactly.

Key Signatures

Key signatures are sharps or flats at the start of each stave and show which scale is being used in the music.

A key signature of
1 sharp is F#
2 sharps is F# C#
3 sharps is F# C# G#.

A key signature of
1 flat is B♭
2 flats is B♭ E♭
3 flats is B♭ E♭ A♭.

The key of C major has no sharps or flats.

The key of G major has one sharp, F#.

The key of F major has one flat, B♭.

The key of D major has two sharps, F# and C#.

The key of B♭ major has two flats, B♭ and E♭.

Join the key name to the key signature.

G major   C major   F major   D major   B♭ major

No sharps or flats   F# C#   B♭ E♭   F#   B♭

Write the key signatures.

G major   D major

In what key is this phrase? ....

In what key is this phrase? ....

Write the treble clef and the key signature for the scales that start on these notes.

Write the treble clef, the key signature and the scale of G major ascending.

Write the treble clef, the key signature and the scale of D major ascending.

Sometimes the key of a tune or phrase is shown by accidentals, perhaps because it has changed key.

Write the key of these phrases.

Write a phrase in G major that includes accidentals. Start and finish on G.

More Major Scales

F major scale (one octave) ascending (B♭)

tone   tone   semitone   tone   tone   tone   semitone

F major scale (one octave) descending (B♭)

Draw a bracket above the semitone intervals.

B♭ major scale (one octave) ascending (B♭ E♭)

Draw a bracket above the semitone intervals.

B♭ major scale (one octave) descending (B♭ E♭)

Draw a bracket above the semitone intervals.

Write in the missing notes and name these scales.

F ....

Write a phrase in F major that includes accidentals. Start and finish on F.

Write in the missing notes and name these scales.

Write the scale of F major ascending.

Write the scale of B♭ major one octave ascending.

Write a phrase in B♭ major that includes accidentals. Start and finish on B♭.

Dotted Crotchets

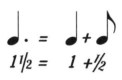

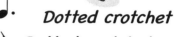

- ♩. Dotted crotchet
- ♩. Dotted crotchet rest

A dot after a note adds half its value to that note.

♩. = ♩ + ♪

1½ = 1 + ½

♩. = ♪ + ♪ + ♪

1½ = ½ + ½ + ½

A dotted crotchet is often followed by a quaver. Together they add up to 2 crotchets.

1   2   +   3   4

Add up the notes and match them to the counts.

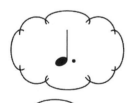

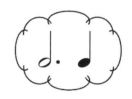

| 2 | 1½ | 4 |

 Write a dotted crotchet rhythm in each bar.

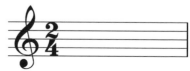

✏ Write the number of beats in the box.

𝗈 = ☐ crotchets

𝗈· = ☐ minims

♩ = ☐ quavers

♩ = ☐ quavers

𝗈· = ☐ crotchets

♩· = ☐ crotchets

♩· = ☐ crotchets

♩· = ☐ quavers

♩· = ☐ quavers

✏ Write in the missing crotchet counts.

1 2 + ... 3 4 1 + ... + 1 ....

✏ Copy the above tune exactly.

✏ Write a phrase that includes a dotted crotchet rhythm. Begin and end on G.

✏ Write a phrase that includes a dotted crotchet rhythm. Begin and end on C.

Add a dotted note to make each bar the correct length.

Match the note with the rest of the same length.

Write in the counts.

1 2

Write the scale of G major in dotted crotchets and quavers.

Write the scale of F major in dotted crotchets and quavers.

✎ **Check 3** How much do you remember?

Mix and Match Match the scale with its key signature.

C major scale   F♯

G major scale   B♭

F major scale   No ♯ No ♭

Quick Check Are the key signatures correct? Tick or cross the answers.

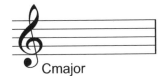
Cmajor

Fmajor

Gmajor

Quiz True or false? Circle the right answer.

1. A dot next to a note doubles the note in length.   True   False

2. Key signatures are written at the start of a line.   True   False

3. The scale of G major has B flat.   True   False

4. Semitones and tones are steps between notes.   True   False

5. All major scales have different patterns of tones and semitones.

                                                True   False

How many did you get right?

Degrees of the Scale

Degrees of the Scale
The first note of a scale is the keynote or 1st degree. The second note is the 2nd degree and the third is the 3rd degree. This contunues until the 8th degree or octave.

So the third degree in C major is the note E.

Degrees of the Scale

C major

| 1st | 2nd | 3rd | 4th | 5th | 6th | 7th | 8th |
| Keynote | | | | | | | Octave |

Write the degree of the scale in the key of C major.

example

3rd   5th   1st   8th

Write the degree of the scale in the key of F major. (F is the 1st degree)

example

8th   4th   6th   2nd

Write the degree of the scale in the key of G major. (G is the 1st degree)

example

2nd   3rd   8th   5th

Write a phrase in C major using only the 1st, 2nd, 3rd and 5th degrees of the scale.

Write a phrase in C major using only the 8th, 6th, 5th and 4th degrees of the scale.

Intervals

Match the interval with its description.

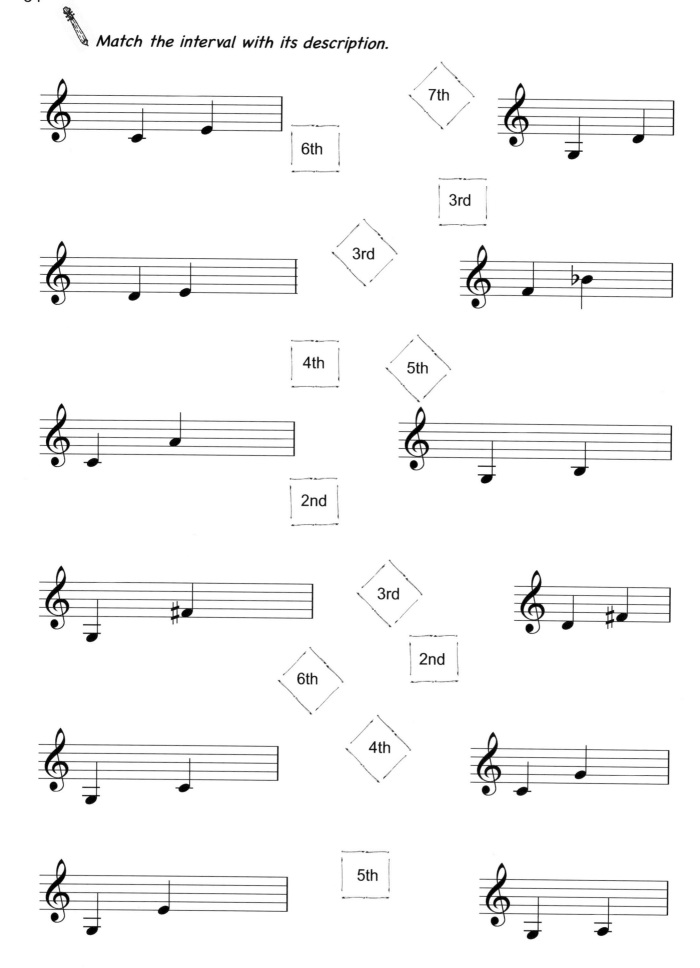

Minor Scales

Relatives
Each minor scale shares a key signature with a major scale. They are related.

The relative minor keynote is the sixth note of the major scale.

There are three kinds of minor scale. They are:
the natural minor scale,
the harmonic minor scale,
the melodic minor scale.
(In Book 2)

The natural minor scale has exactly the same notes as its relative major. But it starts on the 6th note of the major scale.

In C major, the sixth note of the scale is A. So A minor is the relative minor.

A natural minor scale (relative major is C major)

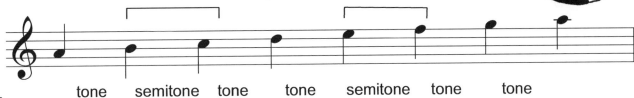

tone   semitone   tone   tone   semitone   tone   tone

Draw a bracket above the semitone intervals.

D natural minor scale (relative major is F major)

Draw a bracket above the semitone intervals.

E natural minor scale (relative major is G major)

Write a phrase using only the notes of the A natural minor scale. Begin and end on A.

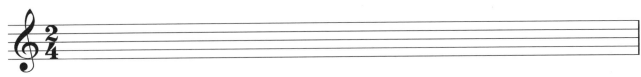

Write in the missing notes and name the scale.

Write in the A natural minor scale ascending and descending.

Write in the E natural minor scale ascending and descending.

Pair up the minor key with its key signature and relative major.

C major

F major

G major

D minor

E minor

A minor

F♯

No sharps or flats

B♭

Harmonic Minor Scales

The harmonic minor scale is the same as the natural minor but the 7th degree is raised by one semitone.

In A natural minor scale the 7th note is G, and becomes G# in the harmonic minor.

Write a # by the 7th degree and complete the scale name.

.... harmonic minor scale

D harmonic .... scale

E .... minor scale

Write in the A harmonic minor scale ascending and descending.

Write in the D harmonic minor scale ascending and descending.

Arpeggios

Arpeggios are made from the 1st, 3rd, 5th and 8th degrees of the scale.

Major and minor arpeggios are made in the same way.

The interval between the 1st and 3rd notes in a minor scale is called a minor 3rd and is made up of three semitones.

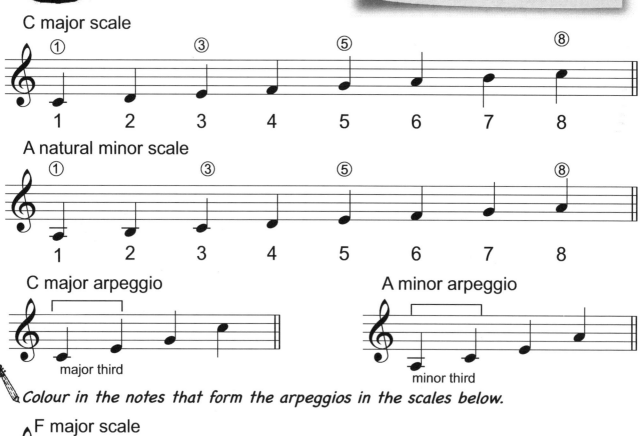

C major scale

① ③ ⑤ ⑧

1 2 3 4 5 6 7 8

A natural minor scale

① ③ ⑤ ⑧

1 2 3 4 5 6 7 8

C major arpeggio

major third

A minor arpeggio

minor third

Colour in the notes that form the arpeggios in the scales below.

F major scale

G major scale

Remember to count from the lowest note of the scale.

 Colour in the notes that form the arpeggios in the scales below.

C major scale

D natural minor scale

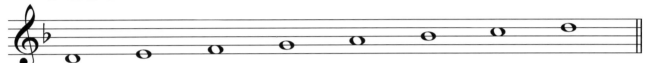

 Write the arpeggio with its key signature. Use any note value.

F major   D minor

G major   E minor

Write a phrase using only the notes from C major arpeggio.

Write a phrase using only the notes from D minor arpeggio.

Write a phrase using only the notes from G major arpeggio.

✎ Check 4 How much do you remember?

Hurray! You're well on your way now

Mix and Match Match the scale with its key signature.

A minor scale   F#

E minor scale   B♭

D minor scale   No # No ♭

Quick Check Are the arpeggios correct? Tick or cross them.

A minor arpeggio

G major arpeggio

F major arpeggio

Quiz True or false? Circle the right answer.

1. A natural minor scale has exactly the same notes as C major scale.

    True   False

2. An octopus is an interval of eight notes.   True   False

3. Each minor scale shares a key signature with a major scale.   True   False

4. Arpeggios are made from the 1st, 3rd, 5th and 7th notes of a scale.   True   False

5. D minor and F major share a key signature.   True   False

How many did you get right?

Musical Symbols

In music, symbols are used to show musical detail e.g. whether to play loud or quiet (dynamics) or how to bow, and many others. Here are a few of the most commonly used.

gradually louder

gradually quieter

Bowing

V   Up-bow (bow travels from point to frog)

⊓   Down-bow (bow travels from frog to point)

,   Bow lift (lift the bow and return it to its starting point)

Slur -joined smoothly

Fermata - pause on the note

Phrase mark - showing one musical phrase

Accent - stressed, strongly

Staccato - short, detached

Tenuto - held and given pressure, broadly

Trill- alternate rapidly to the note above

Musical Terms

Italian words are often used in music to show tempo (speed), dynamics (louds and softs) and directions. Many of them are abbreviated. Here are some of the most commonly used.

accelerando / accel. - *gradually faster*

adagio - *slow*

allegretto - *fairly fast (but not as fast as allegro)*

allegro - *fast*

andante - *at a medium (walking) speed*

crescendo / cresc. - *gradually louder*

da capo / D.C. - *repeat from the beginning*

dal segno / D.S. - *repeat from the sign*

decrescendo / decresc. - *gradually quieter*

diminuendo / dim. - *gradually quieter*

dolce - *sweetly*

fine - *the end*

f **/ forte** - *loud*

ff **/ fortissimo** - *very loud*

grazioso - *graceful*

largo - *slow, stately*

legato - *smoothly*

mezzo - *moderately*

mf **/ mezzo forte** - *moderately loud*

mp **/ mezzo piano** - *moderately quiet*

moderato - *moderately*

p **/ piano** - *quiet*

pp **/ pianissimo** - *very quiet*

presto - *fast*

rallentando / rall. - *gradually slower*

ritenuto / rit. - *held back*

tempo - *speed, time (a tempo - in time)*

vivace - *lively, fast*

Bowing and Special Effects

arco - *play with the bow (often used after a pizzicato section)*

au talon - *play with the bow at the frog*

col legno - *'with the wood' – strike the string with the stick of the bow rather than the hair*

pizzicato - *plucked instead of bowed*

punta d'arco - *bow at the point of the bow*

sul ponticello - *play with the bow near the bridge*

Metronome Marking

♩ = **76** *76 crotchets in a minute*

43

Rearrange these dynamic markings from quietest to loudest.

p f mf ff pp mp

....

Join the term, abbreviation and symbol to its description.

rallentando			crescendo
cresc.	gradually quieter	gradually louder	rall.
accel.			accelerando
diminuendo	gradually slower	gradually faster	dim.

Write the symbol.

Staccato   Accent   Down-bow   Fermata

Add symbols and dynamics to this phrase of music. Be as creative as you like!

Write a phrase that changes tempo gradually.

Write a phrase that changes dynamic gradually.

Repeats and Directions

Repeat from the beginning

Repeat the section

D.S. *Dal Segno*   Repeat from the sign

𝄋   *Segno*   Sign

D.S. al Coda   Repeat from the sign and then play the Coda

⊕   *Coda*   A coda is a phrase that ends a piece of music.

D.C.   *Da Capo*   Go back to the beginning

D.C. al Fine   Go back to the beginning and play to Fine

First-time Bars and Second-time Bars

When a composer wants a tune to be repeated but with a different ending the second time, he or she might use First-time Bars and Second-time Bars instead of writing out the tune in full.

First-time ending (play this the first time)

Stomping like an old moose

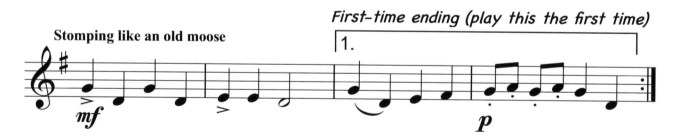

Second-time ending (on the repeat, play this ending instead)

Create a trail. Draw arrows to show where you go and explain the dynamic markings.

Dizzy Demon
from our Demon Studies book

Chipper and dandy with the world spinning

last time go to Coda

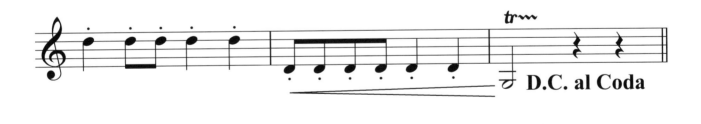

Check 5 How much do you remember?

Fantastic work! You've nearly finished. What a mover!

Mix and Match Match the term with its definition.

D.S.	moderately loud
D.C.	gradually faster
pp	gradually quieter
mf	gradually slower
Allegro	at a medium (walking) speed
Andante	gradually louder
diminuendo	repeat from the beginning
crescendo	very quiet
rallentando	repeat from the sign
accelerando	quick

Quick Check Are the symbols correct? Tick or cross them.

Staccato

Accent   Slur

Pause   Tenuto

Quiz True or false? Circle the right answer.

1. D.C. means go back to the sign.   True   False

2. Trills move from the written note to the note below.   True   False

3. *Fine* means 'the beginning'.   True   False

4. An accent is shown by a little arrow.   True   False

5. A staccato note is shown by a dot.   True   False

6. First and Second-time Bars are different endings.   True   False

7. D.S. means go back to the beginning.   True   False

How many did you get right?

The Violin

How well do you know your violin?

Draw arrows to the parts of the violin and bow.

Scroll

Tuning Pegs

Pegbox

Bridge

Fine tuners

Tailpiece

Lower bout

Neck

Fingerboard

Front / Top

Upper bout

F-holes

Strings

Chinrest

Winding / Wrapping

Eye

Ferrule

Tension screw

Frog / Heel

Stick

Bow hair

Head

Headplate

Tip or point

Violin Care

*After playing, loosen your bow, and dust the rosin off your violin with a soft cloth, checking under the strings and close to the bridge where rosin can easily build up.

*Remember to wipe the fingerboard and strings, and try not to play if you have sticky fingers!

*Avoid touching the bow hair because oil from your skin will stop the bow from playing well.

*Always pick up the bow by its frog, remembering to loosen the hair after each playing to let it rest and keep the bow from warping.

The Range of the Violin

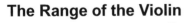

The Violin Family

Today's Violins

Modern violin

Ultra-modern violin

Modern Baroque violin

Electric violins

The violin family also includes the viola, cello and double bass.

Ancestors of the Violin

Lira da braccio   Rebec

Medieval fiddle   Hardanger fiddle

Famous Violins

The 'Messiah' violin made by the Stradivari workshop in 1716 and now in the Ashmolean Museum, Oxford.

'Il Cannone Guarneri' made by the Guarneri workshop in 1743 was played by Paganini and is now in the town hall of Genoa, Italy.

'Le Marien' Stradivarius violin of 1714 was stolen in Manhatten, New York in 2002. It has never been found.

The String Family

Circle the instrument that is not a member of the string family.

Violin

Viola

Cello

Harp

Double Bass

Guitar

Piano

Interesting Violin Facts

The world record in cycling backwards playing a violin is 60.45 kilometres in 5 hours 8 seconds.

Famous people who played the violin include: Albert Einstein (physicist), Charlie Chaplin (actor), Thomas Jefferson (U.S. president), Marlene Dietrich (singer), Michael Angarano (actor), Chris Rankin (actor), Henri Rousseau (artist), Dolly Parton (singer), David Bowie (singer), Louis Farrakahn (activist), Paul Klee (artist), Jayne Mansfield (actor), and Henry Ford (industrialist).

The worlds smallest violin is only 37 millimetres long and is small enough to fit in a box of matches.

Currently, the most expensive violin, is the Vieuxtemps Guarneri, made by Guarneri in 1741, which was sold for over £12 million in 2013. It had been played by Yehudi Menuhin among others. Its anonymous buyer has lent it to concert violinist, Anne Akiko Meyers.

Originally violin strings were made out of sheep gut, (but called catgut) now some strings have a nylon core wound in metal, others are steel wires wound with metal. The windings can be made of aluminium, silver, tungsten, chrome-steel or even gold.

The best quality bow hair comes from stallions from Mongolia, Siberia and Canada where the cold weather makes the hair stronger. It is usually black. White bow hair is usually bleached.

Violins are usually made with a spruce top and a maple back, neck and sides, ebony fingerboard, and rosewood, ebony or boxwood pegs and tailpiece. More expensive violins have a hand-carved back and top and the wood is selected for its pattern and its potential for a great sound.

Purfling is the decorative inlay on the top and back of most violins. It is a sort of reinforcement, and can stop cracks and limit damage if a violin is bumped or knocked.

Rosin comes from sap that is tapped from conifer trees. The resin is heated and ingredients such as: essential oils, beeswax, gold, silver, tin or iron are added to a secret recipe. Violin rosin is designed to suit the violin's strings and is not as sticky as cello or double bass rosin.

Bows are often made from Brazilwood or Pernambuco. Both are woods and come from the same tree but Pernambuco is from the dense heartwood of the tree and produces a bow that can withstand greater tension.

The 'guage' of a string means 'thickness' and it affects the loudness and tone quality A thicker string will be louder and slower to respond. Strings are produced in three guages: light, medium and heavy.

Final Check

Wordsearch

```
C D H Y A N D A N T E K I M D
O D N E C S E R C P T T P E L
C K G R A Z I O S O E G C O T
A O F S E V Z K T N O R M T V
B K D C V I P A U T E I L U I
O B L N W O C T A S S A O N V
F O R T E C O T C S R T M E A
D R I N A U R E I G T B I T C
A U X T A O N T O E E M S I E
L L S J P D R I R W A G S R Y
E S L E O O B G M R K M I P A
G C B E F T E P C I E P N I R
A L A B G L T A P Z D J A A W
T E S H L R T V Z T V N I N E
O F S A C O O O T S E R P O L
```

Can you find these words?

ALLEGRETTO	LEGATO
ALLEGRO	MEZZO
ANDANTE	PIANO
BASS	PIANISSIMO
CLEF	PRESTO
CRESCENDO	RITENUTO
DECRESCENDO	SLUR
DIMINUENDO	STACCATO
DOLCE	TENUTO
FORTE	VIVACE
FORTISSIMO	
GRAZIOSO	
LARGO	

Can you find these words?

BOW
BRIDGE
DOWNBOW
FERRULE
FHOLES
FINGERBOARD
FROG
GAUGE
GUARNERI
HARDANGER
LIRADABRACCIO
MAPLE
PEGS
PERNAMBUCO
PURFLING
REBEC
ROSIN
SCROLL
SHEEPGUT
STRADIVARIUS

```
        A S Q Q              E X R G
      E L D Q G L          U L A Y O P
      P B I Z S D Q R      L W P N G F S Y
    O R E F E Q N Z T I  Q K W A Q E P Z I Q
    Z H U O C E T L B D  Q L H H M B K K X H N Q
    L S C R O L L H A R D A N G E R L B S Y B M S A
    I C Q G I S C E F R O G B P F H O L E S L J G F
    D L Z Z K P T N X X L I R A D A B R A C C I O N
    E R J E C U E R A J E G U A G B C U Z H Z X E M
    J G D I E H S R A M B D O W N B O W K W C L K X
    I U D W B L Y Y N D R K C F I N G E R B O A R D
    R X I E M K Q P A I U E M S R F M I D A B R
    J E S R O Z N Y I M V R Q V M T K I L Z L Z
      O N H B L A J S S B A G E L U R R E F H
      X R E F M R G G G U R B U G U R R W
      B A E H E S D N U C I I E R T R
      Z U P Y I X I L Q O U B C V
      H G G N W L J N S P S X
      H X U Y F D W B T E
      B V T R O D B A
      A J U O T X
      F P C H
      G I
```

Wow!
Congratulations!
You've finished.
What a great
achievement.

The Violinist's Progress

Tick the box for each topic completed.

☐ Treble Clef

☐ Letter Names

☐ Note Values

☐ Stems

☐ Rests

☐ Check 1

☐ Time Signatures

☐ Accidentals

☐ Quavers

☐ Ledger Lines

☐ Check 2

☐ Major Scales

☐ Key Signatures

☐ More Major Scales

☐ Dotted Crotchets

☐ Check 3

☐ Degrees of the Scale

☐ Intervals

☐ Minor Scales

☐ Arpeggios

☐ Check 4

☐ Musical Symbols

☐ Musical Terms

☐ Repeats and Directions

☐ Check 5

☐ The Violin

☐ The Violin Family

☐ The String Family

☐ Interesting Violin Facts

☐ Final Check

Congratulations

to

....

for completing

The Vibrant Violin Music Theory Book 1!

If you have enjoyed **The Vibrant Violin Music Theory Book 1** why not try the other books in the **Vibrant Violin** series!

For more info, please visit: **WildMusicPublications.com**

All of our books are available to download, or you can order from Amazon.

Introducing some of our favourites:

Violin Practice Notebook

50+ Greatest Classics

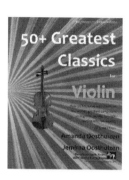

Christmas Carols

Trick or Treat – A Halloween Suite

Intermediate Classic Duets

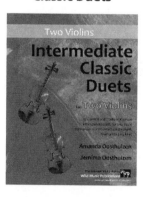

Fish 'n' Ships

Easy Duets from Around the World

Christmas Duets

Violin Music Theory Book 2

Christmas Duets for Violin and Viola

Easy Traditional Duets for Flute and Violin

Intermediate Classic Duets for Descant Recorder and Violin

More Christmas Duets for Violin and Cello

Very Easy Christmas Duets for Teacher and Pupil

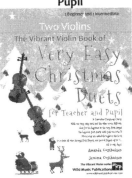

Champagne and Chocolate

Moonlight and Roses

Christmas Crackers

Easy Tunes from Around the World

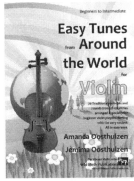

Christmas Bonanza

Easy Classic Duets

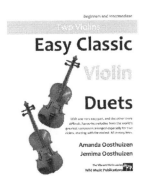

Easy Traditional Duets

Printed in Great Britain
by Amazon